First published in the UK in 2016

© 2016 Emily Webber

ISBN-13: 978 0 9574919 3 9

Published by Drew London Ltd.

Design and typesetting by Drew London Ltd.

Building successful communities of practice Discover how learning together makes better organisations

Contents

Introduction

Our natural human desire is to connect with other people and to seek out a sense of belonging. People need to feel supported. Because of this, communities naturally develop in many places.

Business organisations are no different. People who don't feel supported in their jobs don't stay around for long, or if they do, they are unmotivated and unhappy. In a time where organisational structures and culture changes so rapidly, helping people connect and feel supported is more important than ever.

Throughout my professional career and my personal life, I have been involved in building and leading different types of communities, including:

- communities of interest: people who meet around a shared passion. For example, meetup groups for people interested in film

- communities of place: people who have a connection through the area they live in. For example, a residents association or a local web forum

- communities of action: people who gather around a cause or specific event. For example, objecting to building plans

- communities of practice: "…groups of people who share a concern or a passion for something they do and learn how to do it better as they interact regularly" (Etienne Wenger-Trayner and Beverly Wenger-Trayner) [1]

Sometimes this has been for personal motivations. At other times, it has been to make a difference for others. I have had some great successes with communities and I have written this book to share what has worked for me with you.

There are many other types of communities, but this book will focus specifically on communities of practice in the business organisation, drawing from my own experience in the subject.

I have experienced first hand that communities of practice can: support organisational learning; accelerate professional development of their members; enable knowledge sharing and management; support better communication; build better practices; make people happier; break down silos; and help with hiring and retention or staff.

The community of practice is not a new concept. The name was first published by cognitive anthropologists Jean Lave and Etienne Wenger in 1991[2], and connecting people through their practice in and out of organisations has been around as long as people have been in organisations. I have witnessed a current increasing interest in communities of practice in business organisations, which could be attributed a number of factors including: the rise in organisations using management techniques that encourage learning, promote transparency and break down traditional hierarchy structures; the increase in quality technology that allows people to connect and collaborate over long distances; and the reduction in budgets committed to professional learning.

The secret to a resilient, happy organisation is to be one that invests in learning and development of its people and its whole. This book will help you on your way to creating your own self-sustaining community of practice to support that learning and development.

This book draws on personal experience and research into successful communities of practice. Advice within it is taken from techniques that I have found to work for me within organisations.

It's important to remember that each situation is different; what works in one place, may not work in another, so always be open to changing the approach if something does not work for you.

Who is this book for?

This book is a concise guide for anyone who wants to improve working life for themselves and others in their organisation or across organisations:

- if you have ever felt unsupported and frustrated at work, feeling like you are expected to have all the answers and no one to talk ideas through with or to give you feedback

- if you are leading a department, organisation or profession and want to create ways for people to learn and help them love their work

- if you are in charge of learning and development, or training budgets, and are looking for ways to get more value for staff

- if you are responsible for line management, hiring and professional development and want to find ways to support growing talent within your organisation rather than always turning to contractors or suppliers

- if you want to find ways to get a deeper understanding and knowledge of what you do by connecting with others like you

then this book is for you.

What you'll see throughout the book

Throughout this book, I'll share advice drawn from my own experience of building communities of practice. I will also cite research by others. I will give practical guidance that you can try for yourself and that has worked for me in the past. I'll take you through early stages, through to a successful self-sustaining community, talking about things to consider along the way.

It's worth remembering that no community is the same; it takes hard work, a willingness to try things out and a lot of enthusiasm. But the return on your investment will be worth it.

1. Why You Need Communities of Practice in Your Organisation

There are many benefits that come from having a successful community of practice. In this chapter I'll highlight some of those I've found most valuable in my own work. If you have picked up this book, then you should see some parallels to help you articulate the need within your own organisation.

These benefits are:

- accelerating professional development across the organisation

- breaking down organisational silos

- sharing knowledge and building better practice

- hiring and building a better team

- happier, more motivated people

Accelerating Professional Development Across the Organisation

When I talk to people about training, I like to remind them that training and learning are not the same thing. You take part in training, but that does not mean that you will learn.

Many people and organisations think about training when they think about learning and professional development. This often equates to a personal training budget for courses and events. This not only means that people have an individualistic experience of professional development — they do it in isolation from their peers — but also means there is a lack of consideration for the ongoing support needed to take the knowledge and turn it into experience.

> "Knowledge is something you buy with the money. Wisdom is something you acquire by doing it" (Taiichi Ohno 1988) [3]

Although training courses and events can be valuable, particularly when the focus is on the development of a particular skill, it should be viewed as one element of how we gain knowledge. It should not be the sole way for people to develop skills. Learning does not end with the taking of a test or the confirmation that someone has sat through a day-long training session. We also learn from other people and we learn by doing.

Social Learning, learning from other people

Social learning is learning within a social context.

> "Most human behavior is learned observationally through modeling: from observing others one forms an idea of how new behaviors are performed, and on later occasions this coded information serves as a guide for action." [4] (Albert Bandura 1971)

This stems from how we learn as children. We initially learn through mirroring what we see other people doing, which when put into practice becomes experience and part of our own behaviour.

Because communities of practice have social interactions at their core, they naturally take advantage of social learning between members.

Experiential Learning, learning by doing

To get the full benefit of classroom training and social learning, people need the chance to put concepts and principles into action and to learn from their subsequent experiences.

David Kolb describes learning as:

> "The process whereby knowledge is created through the transformation of experience" [5]

In his research Kolb created a model of learning styles, which specifically states that learning cannot happen without active experimentation with new knowledge.

CONCRETE EXPERIENCE

Having a new experience

REFLECTIVE OBSERVATION

Reflection on that experience

ABSTRACT CONCEPTUALISATION

Concluding and learning from the experience

ACTIVE EXPERIMENTATION

Trying out what you've learnt

Kolb's learning styles model

Communities of practice give people opportunities to experiment with what they have learnt, in a safe environment and with the support of other people.

A rounded curriculum for learning

In 2014, I created some guidance on a rounded curriculum for learning, published in the Government Service Design Manual [6]. I wanted to be able to point to this guidance when asked about how people learn Agile development [7], which was new for many people across government. My assumption was that most people who were professionals in the area had not been formally trained, as it was not something that was available at schools or colleges, and so they had learnt through a series of comparable experiences. For the guidance I wanted to explore if this was true, and to discover what career experiences had led them to this point.

I gathered together a group of professionals with a range of experience and facilitated a workshop. During the session, I asked us to each map out our own personal learning journeys, from the moment we first heard about the topic until the present day. We shared these with the rest of the group and through that process identified experiences that we felt had influenced our learning journey.

There were some common themes that arose. These included the need to change how we worked due to frustrations, our own research on the topic, times we had come up against difficult situations and worked through them and how we had connected with other people to help them learn. Much of this was rooted in social and experiential learning, with the added factor of personal motivation.

I used what came out of the session to write the guidance, which now serves as a reference for government departments and interested people. It lays out a set of learning activities that create a more rounded curriculum than most organisations offer. It is as follows:

- shadowing people and learning from others

- formal classroom training

- self-initiated learning (networking and speaking to other professionals, reading blogs and books)

- sharing ideas and support from others (talking to other people, writing blog posts and public speaking)

- small experiments and running short projects

- questioning, retrospecting and feedback loops

Having a community of practice in place can support many of these ways of learning. A community will create the connections for shadowing, and will help people build their own classroom learning curriculum through recommendation and even taking classes together. Members will share their own self-initiated learning with each other, share ideas with each other, and support each other while trying out new techniques. The support network of a community will create the safe environment in which to try out new things, as well as creating social motivation among its members to learn.

Communities of practice create the right environment for social learning, experiential learning and a rounded curriculum, leading to accelerated learning for members. This is vital in professional areas because traditional learning methods cannot provide the real experience to back up more traditional training. It can encourage a learning culture where people seek better ways to do things, rather than only using existing models.

Breaking Down Organisational Silos

Silos can form where a group of people feel a deeper loyalty to each other than to other groups of people. They can happen between organisations, or within organisations between functions, departments, programmes, teams and other groups. Communication between silos can be very difficult, causing duplication of work and frustration for those inside them. Silos can be very damaging to an organisation.

Communities that span these silos can go a long way to breaking those barriers down and creating a better appreciation for how others work, improving communication and workflow.

Imagine a scenario where a Sara, a developer from team A, has to work with code produced by team B. She finds the code is formatted in a way that she doesn't like, so she spends much of her time reformatting it. Sara often talks about it to her fellow team members. She might be heard saying:

> "Team B are not very good developers.
> We are always correcting their code."

There may be many good reasons why their code is formatted in this way; for example, they may not know a better way of doing it, or they may have constraints that are unclear to Sara. If Sara got to know the developers on the other team, she would start to see them as people rather than just 'Team B'. She would start to understand their own situation and could offer to help them with code formatting.

If Sara and the Team B developers were within a community of practice, this introduction would have already been made. They would just work together.

Sharing Knowledge and Building Better Practice

Organisations have been trying to manage knowledge for as long as the workforce moved to knowledge work. This practice of knowledge management is defined as a way to capture what people know about a topic in order to transfer it through people changes; inform others; identify important practices; and minimise loss of corporate memory.

Knowledge management is often 'solved' with technology. How many times have you come across a company wiki, social network or document storage system? And how often is that system out of date, confusing or not relevant to your work? Without a team of people keeping knowledge management stores up to date, and adding new content, they start to become redundant very quickly. People begin to mistrust them and they become abandoned. This is just a waste of time and money.

This type of knowledge management only accounts for information that is easy to share and write down. There is more to knowledge than this. It is not as tangible and easily documented as it might seem. There is a huge amount of knowledge that is not able to be documented. This is referred to as tacit knowledge, knowledge which is implicit in people's actions, rather than explicit knowledge, knowledge that lives in repeatable process and can be written down.

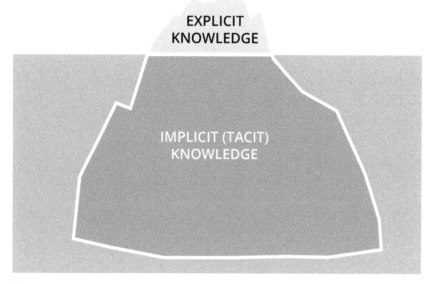

Knowledge as an iceberg

Tacit knowledge is described by Cook and Brown [8] as Knowing, where explicit knowledge is Knowledge. They state that these two types of information should be treated very differently. Wenger, McDermott and Snyder refer to tacit knowledge as Practice, where explicit knowledge is Process. This definition supports a theory of experiential learning, where knowledge is a process that can be told, but practice is the experience of that knowledge.

Consider riding a bike: you can understand the process of riding a bike, be told how physics and balance keep you upright, and how peddling drives the wheels to move you forward. But unless you understand the practice of riding a bike — actually getting on it and moving forwards — it will be almost impossible for you to do.

Tacit knowledge is hard to write down or visualise, and so is very difficult to document. This makes it hard to capture and share in formal or explicit ways. But it is often shared between communities and forms an integral part of their culture.

It is vital to retain tacit knowledge. According to Jeanne Meister [9], people don't stay in jobs for life; they move around on average every 4.4 years. (For those born between the early 1980s and 2000s, even more often.) An organisation that doesn't support the sharing of tacit knowledge will lose most of their knowledge as people move on.

As a community of practice matures, it starts to take ownership of its own processes and practices. Supporting structures that underpin the sharing of knowledge make any organisation or community more resilient to changes in its members.

Building better practice

Bringing together a diverse group of people that share the same challenges, but have different experiences, creates a wider pool of knowledge to draw from when it comes to problem-solving.

As a community matures, it will move on from just sharing knowledge to solving shared problems, using the collective knowledge of the community. This will create better practice. The community working together will lead to better knowledge retention and to continuing to seek better solutions to similar issues. This creates better ways of working for an organisation.

Later on in this book, I cover ways to encourage people to work together to share problem-solving.

Hiring and Building a Better Team

If you have established communities of practice, hiring new skills into an organisation becomes easier.

If the professional community you are hiring into can clearly articulate its values, you have a set of criteria to help identify who is a good fit for the role that the community represents. If they can identify skills gaps and development needs, then you have an understanding of what skills a person would need to fill those gaps.

Once a new person joins, the community acts as a support network, so that they can quickly acclimatise to the organisation's culture and purpose.

Good community skills distribution

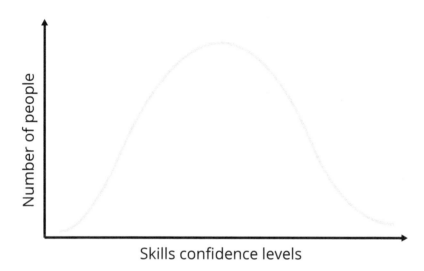

Good community skills distribution

Having well-distributed skills confidence levels across a group can give you the capacity to bring in less experienced people with a view to developing their skills through support from the community.

Broadly, most of the community should be in the intermediate skills confidence area, with some specialisms. Part of your community will be in the high skills confidence area, if you have contractors or consultants they will most likely be here. As long as you have a good spread in these areas, you can start to bring in more entry-level or junior staff who have greater development needs. This helps to build a sustainable workforce.

I have seen organisations where most people are in the lower skill set area, particularly organisations that are taking on new types of work. This creates an environment where everyone is learning together; and without any expert input, it can create a large development overhead and slow down the learning process for everyone. Where I have seen this, I've worked with them to bring in more people with an intermediate or high level of skills, to help balance, while focusing on how they will upskill existing staff.

In order to do this, you might want to carry out a skills audit with the community to identify what skills exist and what level people are at. I talk more about identifying and growing skills in chapter 8, 'Identifying Skills Gaps to Work On'.

Happier, More Motivated People

We instinctively know that happier people do better work and are more motivated. 'Happiness and Productivity' [10] a study by Andrew J. Oswald, Eugenio Proto, and Daniel Sgroi, showed that happiness made people 12% more productive. Because of this, happiness is something that companies like Google [11] incorporate into their working practices. The study illustrated that the happier people were, the more motivation they exhibited.

According to Dan Pink [12], what motivates us has changed; the idea of reward-based motivation, otherwise known as extrinsic motivation, no longer applies in value-added work. We spend a large proportion of our lives at work. We want to be fulfilled by what we do, by intrinsic motivation. Pink categorises this into three points of motivation:

- autonomy — the desire to direct our own lives

- mastery — the urge to get better and better at something that matters

- purpose — the yearning to do what we do in the service of something larger than ourselves

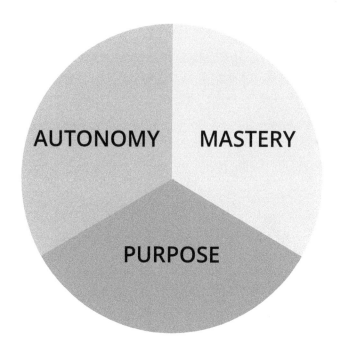

Dan Pink's three aspects of motivation

This follows on from work by Ryff and Keyes [13] which highlights six points of motivation:

- autonomy

- environmental Mastery

- personal Growth

- positive Relations with Others

- purpose in Life

- self-acceptance

Communities of practice can support a number of these points of motivation, including the mastery of craft and personal growth, as well as positive relations with others. Through formal and informal activities, the community can benefit from social learning. Members get better together, raising the skill level of everyone in the community.

Bringing people into a supportive community fosters positive relations with others and creates a feeling of acceptance. Communities of practice can play an important part in helping to increase the happiness of their members.

2. The Stages of a Community of Practice

A community takes time and dedication to grow, and passes through a number of stages as it does. During these stages, it has different support needs and different energy levels. It's valuable to be mindful of where the community is in its development process to help understand how you can best support it.

Etienne Wenger, Richard McDermott and William M. Snyder mapped out these stages in their 2002 book, 'Cultivating Communities of Practice — A Guide to Managing Knowledge' [14]. Their model echoes what I have seen in practice and has helped me better understand the communities I have been involved in building. In the diagram below I have also plotted the energy input needed to build and sustain a community at every stage, either from a leader or sponsor of the community. This is also highlighted in the 'Community of Practice Maturity Model' in the Appendix.

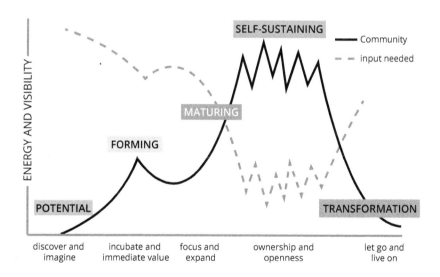

Adapted from stages of community development
(Wenger, McDermott and Snyder)

The stages of a community of practice are:

- potential
- forming
- maturing
- self-sustaining
- transformation

Potential

The community will typically begin life as loose networks (or individuals) that hold the potential of becoming more connected. Energy levels of the members are low at this point, but will start to increase.

A large input of focus and support from the community leader(s) is needed at this stage.

Forming

As members build connections and relationships with each other, they start to come together into a community. They will be exploring opportunities at this stage, and there will be an increase in members' energy levels as the community builds.

Community leaders need less direct input while this is happening, and should allow the group to form bonds.

Maturing

During this stage, the community will grow in membership, commitment and the depth of knowledge members share. The community will start to form strong bonds and trust. The energy of members may initially dip as the community matures, but will steadily grow.

Community leaders will need more structured input at this stage to support the development of the community.

Self-sustaining

During this stage, the community will have enough momentum and commitment from its members to continue with less effort from a single leader or leadership group. Members will take ownership of the knowledge and practices they create and share. The energy of members during this stage will remain generally high, but experience higher and lower cycles.

During this stage, community leaders will need the least amount of input, as members will adopt part of the leadership role

Transformation

Sometimes a dramatic event; a large part of the community leaves, there's a sudden influx of new members, or a drop in energy. This calls for a radical transformation: perhaps a return to an earlier incubation or growth stage, or even the end of the community.

§

These also echo Tuckman's stages of group development [15]:
'Forming — Storming — Norming — Performing'.

During *forming* the group is getting to know each other; *storming* is when the group starts to identify its boundaries, and where conflicts may arise; *norming* is when they start to gain a rhythm and the relationship matures; and while *performing*, the group has its own momentum and takes responsibility for itself.

See the 'Community of Practice Maturity Model' in the Appendix for more detail on what you would expect to see at each stage of a community's development.

3. Creating the Right Environment

It is important to give a community the best opportunity to succeed. This begins with creating the best environment that you can in order to support it. In this chapter, I discuss how to give your community its best chance to succeed.

This includes:

- the ability to meet regularly

- the right community leadership

- creating a 'safe to fail learn' environment

- getting support from your organisation

The Ability to Meet Regularly

Your community will need to communicate regularly and often. This should be a combination of chances to get together as a group in real time and more asynchronous communication. These opportunities to connect will need to vary in content to help avoid repetition, to aid learning and to encourage discussion. As the community matures, you'll start to identify what it needs as a group.

Your community will have the best chance of building trust between its members if people have the chance to be physically in the same place and are able to meet face-to-face. Spending time with people builds trust far more quickly and successfully than at a distance. If your community members work in the same building, this is far easier than if your members are distributed throughout different offices, the country or the world. If your community is distributed you'll have to work harder to get people together. If meeting up is logistically difficult, then you need to find other ways to connect and build trust. When considering how viable your community is, think about how they will connect on a regular basis. If it is impossible for them to do this, then the community won't work.

If your community is likely to be distributed over a large distance, think about how they will build trust. Try to find a way for them at least to spend some time together in the same space; this will be an extremely valuable exercise in team bonding and supports the transfer of tacit knowledge through less structured conversations. Familiarity and trust is often built through ad hoc conversations, when people start to share things about themselves outside of specific work activities.

If you have groups of people in the community that are distributed over various locations, consider how you could enlist local coordinators in each group to help ensure the community engages across all locations. These co-ordinators can then meet regularly to align on community activities.

You should also consider what technology you have in place to support computer-mediated conversation, such as group emails, instant messaging, collaboration software and video conferencing

The Right Community Leadership

With any community it's important to consider what good leadership looks like. Leadership may come from those wanting to set the community up, or might be someone appointed by the organisation in an attempt to kick-start communities of practice.

These leaders need to be knowledgeable, passionate, respected and empowered.

Depending on the size and scope of the community, it can be a full-time job for one person or split across a number of people. It should not be a role simply added to someone's existing workload. Giving people time to dedicate to it is essential. I have seen communities suffer when their leaders are over-committed elsewhere and project work always ends up taking a higher priority than the community. It is hard for a community to flourish in this context.

Empowering leaders through organisational structure

One way of empowering a community's leadership (and which I have witnessed being successful) is to structure an organisation around its communities of practice.

An organisation that I have previously worked in; Government Digital Service (GDS) has a 'matrix management' structure [16]; communities were created as a response to the growth of the organisation and in order to provide and distribute line management better. Heads of profession were created to ensure consistency and quality across the professions they led. This was my role in the Agile Delivery profession.

As a line manager, I had responsibility for supporting and developing staff. Having a specific reporting line through the community of practice to the head of profession — rather than through a programme or department — ensures the focus of learning and development is related to what every person needs in order to do their job well. It also removes any conflict of interest between personal development and programme demands.

Everyone belongs to a team, which often belongs to a programme which creates direction for day to day work and project related outcomes people are trying to achieve. Everyone also belongs to a community of practice; this creates direction in how each does their work and helps them to do it better.

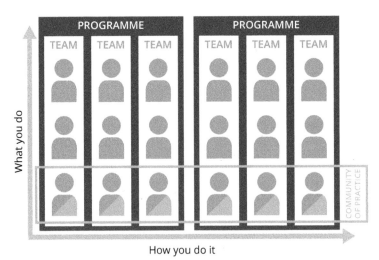

Government Digital Service 'matrix management'

Similarly, music streaming service Spotify created a comparable structure through what they call squads, tribes, chapters and guilds. This model was developed during the scaling of their organisation and has helped them to maintain levels of quality, knowledge and delivery. Their squads equate to teams; tribes equate to programmes or themes; chapters equate to communities of practice; and guilds equate to communities of interest. Again, line management happens through an individual's chapter, rather than their tribe.

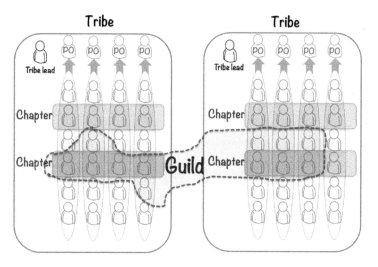

From 'Spotify Engineering Culture part 1' [17]

Even if there is an appointed leader — as in this model — leadership of the community works best if decision-making is distributed among its members. In the next chapter, I cover community leadership in more depth.

Creating a 'Safe to Fail Learn' Environment

Trust is the basis of a successful community of practice, so it is important that the members of the community feel safe with each other. Trust may not come immediately, but with support and time it will develop.

A safe community environment is a place where members believe that whatever their experience, they can contribute and ask questions openly without being judged. In turn, they don't judge others. To have a high-performing community, everyone needs to acknowledge they can always learn from others within the community.

Community members must be welcoming and friendly to new members and must invite questions and discussion without being aggressive. The community leader(s) will make sure any negative or bad behaviour is addressed to keep the environment safe.

Make sure you have a private space where you can close the door and safely talk with each other during regular get-togethers. Be cautious about inviting new people or non-community members into the group, particularly during the early stages.

When you first meet, you can start to discuss how members will act towards each other, which will include some of these points. I talk about things you can do to encourage communication and trust a little later, and when to open the door to other groups later in this book.

Getting Support from Your Organisation

For a community to become high performing, it must benefit from support from the organisation within which it lives.

You may be in a situation where the organisation is actively sponsoring the development of your community. If not, then you can choose to look for support before you start building the community, or look for it once your community is more established. The decision will be based on your own situation and your knowledge of your organisation. Getting up-front support can help establish the community quicker, but may lead to formalising the community too much before its members get to know each other. If you are not sure how supportive the organisation will be, you can put off getting support to give the community a chance to gain some momentum and evidence of its benefits before proving a case.

Whichever way you do it, it will become vital at some point.

Organisational support consists of time, people and money.

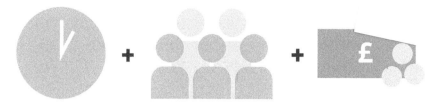

Time

People within the community need time to dedicate to its membership and an acknowledgement of this from the organisation. In an organisation that tracks time or uses timesheets, it may mean creating a specific job code or reducing the billable target to allow for time off from projects.

People

The organisation may also need to appoint people whose job role is to specifically lead or support the community.

Money

It's worth getting hold of a budget allowance for the community, too, to use for travel to meet up, room booking, external speakers, social occasions or tools that the community may need to use.

If your community is not within an organisation, then you will still need time from members, people to lead or guide the community, and money. For example, a meetup might need: time to attend sessions; people to organise the sessions; people to speak; and money to cover refreshments, either from participants or from a sponsor.

4. The Leadership of a Community of Practice

Leading a community of practice differs from more traditional leadership within an organisation, in that communities of practice encourage active participation and decision-making by members as opposed to decision-making by the leader or group of leaders.

In this chapter I look at:

- different types of community leadership

- community leadership roles

Different Types of Community leadership

There are different types of leadership models that a community might follow and that will evolve as members take ownership of the group, which should be encouraged. They are:

- single leader

- shared leadership

- fully co-owned leadership

- distributed leadership

Single leader

Communities may have a single leader appointed by the organisation, the community or themselves.

Within an organisation, it might be part of the management structure and this person may have been hired into the specific role, like the matrix model covered in chapter 3, 'Creating the Right Environment'. This can be a great way of getting the community started, as long as the appointed leader is respected by those in the community and is knowledgeable about community building, or seeks out knowledge to understand. It can hinder the success of the community if she or he is rejected by the community members as a leader. If the community is already partly established, it would be a valuable exercise to ask the community to appoint this person.

The community may choose to appoint a person in a democratic way; this ensures that the community respects the position of the person they have chosen. It's also important that any appointed leader has time and space to take on the role.

In the early days of a community, a person may naturally become the leader by being the person who recognises the need for the community. As long as the community accepts this, there may be no need to change or formalise it any further.

Even if the leader is appointed by an organisation, by the community or by an individual, there is always room for evolving and emerging leadership and sharing of leadership responsibilities. Any single leader should seek opportunities to move towards a shared or co-owned model.

Single, shared and co-owned community leadership

Shared leadership

Another model sees leadership shared among a core group of people. These people may be appointed by the organisation or group, or they may simply have emerged. In this instance, the core group will share leadership responsibilities. As the community evolves, people will move in and out of this core group. Roles and responsibilities will either naturally emerge from interactions or be explicitly defined by the core group.

There may be an additional overhead arising from communication between the group of leaders. The added value is that each person should need less time to dedicate than they would if they were a single leader, and may not need to be solely dedicated to their leadership role.

Fully co-owned leadership

A very committed self-sustaining community may have a fully co-owned leadership model, where everyone in the community takes responsibility for its leadership. As with shared ownership, roles may emerge naturally or need to be defined by the whole community.

Distributed leadership

When a community is distributed over a number of locations, the leadership model should follow this distribution and identify leaders in those locations. This will ensure there is always someone local to all within the community and will encourage involvement right across the distributed community. A distributed leadership may also encompass a single leader, shared leadership or fully co-owned leadership in each of the locations. Like the examples above, this should be allowed to evolve depending on who is involved in each location.

Distributed leadership

Leaders from different locations should come together regularly to ensure alignment.

Community Leadership Roles

Whatever your community leadership structure, there are a number of things that the role must cover in order to create a thriving, valuable community. These are:

- building, sustaining and developing the community

- managing people and dynamics

- community support and facilitation

- informing, advising or coaching members

- defining professional direction and standards

- representing community members within and outside the organisation

Building, sustaining and developing the community

Perhaps one of the most important roles is getting the community going in the first place, and keeping it going. This takes a lot of energy in the early stages and will require different inputs at points throughout the community's life.

Ongoing building of the community encompasses bringing in new members, either through hiring into an organisation, or reaching out to new people that have the potential to be members. It also refers to the development of those members, in terms of relationships between them, the overall professional development of the community and members' own professional development.

Managing people and dynamics

Once a community is mature it will be able to self-manage and will address its own issues with dynamics. But there will be times when someone will need to mediate, particularly for a new community or if new members have recently joined. Your community principles will underpin how the members expect to treat each other, and can help to address any issues.

Having a leader who is good at motivating people will help with community dynamics, as will having someone who ensures that community members remain respectful of each other's experiences.

Community support and facilitation

In order to keep the community active, someone will need to make sure that it regularly communicates and that members are getting value out of their interactions. This role is all about supporting the community in a servant-leader way.

The role of a servant-leader or facilitator is to ensure that the community has everything it needs in order to function. This might cover making sure rooms are booked, removing obstacles that are blocking the community from progressing, and facilitating workshops. The servant-leadership role is most relevant for a mature, high-performing community.

Informing, advising or coaching members

This role may live within the community or alongside it; it may also cross over into the development of community members. It may potentially be linked with line management.

The role of a coach is generally advisory. A coach is there to support individuals or a team on a focused basis. Coaching might be used as and when needed, or may happen on a regular basis. The role of coaching or mentoring doesn't necessarily only happen between a more senior and more junior person. It can also happen on a peer-to-peer level, so might be something that happens across the community.

If a community is distributed, or interacts through computer-mediated conversation, there is a specific role for a facilitator to keep people engaged and forums active. They can help do this by starting conversation topics, responding to questions that members have or encouraging others to join in.

Defining community direction and standards

Those who lead a community should be able to define the direction of that community, through leading the creation of a vision and goals for members. They should also set the standards for what 'good' looks like within the profession at various levels. It helps if anyone involved in this area acts as a good role model and has significant high-level experience to draw upon.

Representing community members within and outside the organisation

There is a place for people to represent the community and its members within an organisation and in the wider environment. This might be in meetings, at workshops, or at networking events. It might take the form of representing the voice and values of the community, or of backing up community members or protecting them to make the space to focus on work.

Whatever model you try, keep reviewing and adapting it based on what is working for the community at different stages in its life cycle.

5. Identifying Who is in the Community

You have identified an organisational and user need for a community and how it will benefit its members. You've sold the concept to your organisation (or at least to a small group of people that are initially keen). Now you want to make it happen. This is the beginning of your journey; there is huge potential. You now need some community members.

I have found that communities thrive best when there is an understanding of the boundaries around membership. These boundaries provide members with the emotional safety necessary for needs and feelings to be exposed and for intimacy to develop. Based on this, I have focused on understanding the boundaries which inform who is invited into the community.

Before you can do this, you'll need to be able to articulate a few things:

- what role or family of roles is this community for?

- are there any existing connections you can build on?

- what are the broad vision and initial goals of the community?

Once you have done this, you will need to identify who belongs in the community and recruit them.

What Role or Family of Roles is this Community For?

You may have already answered this question by the time you reach this point — when you first identified the need. If it is your job to head up a profession within your organisation, you may find this question easy to answer because it's probably part of your job description. If you are an individual wanting to create something for people like you, then you have your answer: it's people like you. If neither of these apply, think about where the need is greatest, and what need you are trying to address with your community.

Are There any Existing Connections You can Build on?

In most organisations where I been involved in setting up a community of practice, there have been pre-existing connections that have great potential to become a community of practice. In your organisation you may be able to identify project managers having a weekly status meeting to talk about issues; software developers who regularly have lunch together; or account managers that get together over a glass of wine to talk about their day. Identifying these existing connections made it easier to build on them. If there isn't a ready-made group, you may find pockets of people already meeting that you can build upon.

People who work in the same place and share the same role often gravitate towards each other, because they seek connections. If there are no ready-made connections within the organisation or potential network, you might want to consider any barriers that have prevented this from happening. These might relate to culture, technology, organisational structure or distance. This is something you can explore with early members as the community starts to build.

At the early stage, you will most likely reach people that you already know or are aware of. As the community starts to mature, you will need to start finding new routes and working harder to reach new people. I talk about this more in chapter 9, 'Growing The Community'.

What Are the Broad Vision and Initial Goals for the Community?

If you are this far down the line, you'll understand the need for the community and this will feed your broad vision for it. Your vision should be aspirational, achievable and easy to understand. You'll find lots of ideas to base this on in chapter 1, 'Why you Need Communities of Practice in your Organisation'. Goals towards that vision should try to be SMART (specific, measurable, achievable, relevant, timely). This helps place constraints around them, which helps people to focus. You don't have to have your goals up-front, as you should involve the community in creating them. But you might have some that are specific to the reason that you wanted to build the community in the first place.

A goal that I have used in the past is to:

Increase knowledge within the permanent staff to reduce the reliance on contractors in the next six months.

This is a clear goal that has a measurable outcome and helped to inform the focus of the community. As a community matures, it will take ownership of its goals and review and update them on a regular basis to make them relevant.

Once you have answered these three points, you can set about inviting members.

Identify Who Belongs in The Community and Recruit Them

You know who the community is for. But identifying precisely who those people are is not always quite so straightforward. Many people share the same role, but have different job titles or are in different parts of an organisation. You'll need to do some work to reach the right people.

In the past, I have written out the names of people who I think might fit, based on what I know about their job titles or roles. I found some people easy to identify; I then asked questions to help me work out people I was unclear about.

When trying to determine who should join, some questions you need to answer are:

- does this person share a role, similar environment and overall work goals with other people in the community? (purpose)

- does this person share the same day-to-day challenges as other people in the community? (challenges)

- would this person be able to learn things from other people in the community that would make them better at their job? (learning)

- would people in the community be able to learn things relevant for their day-to-day work from working closely with this person? (teaching)

Anyone for whom you can answer "yes" to all four questions is someone you want to talk to about joining, articulating why you are asking them and the purpose of the community.

Let's try this with Paula, an IT project manager at XYZ company who we're considering for a community of practice for project managers.

Q: *Does Paula share a role, similar environment and overall goals with other people in the community?*

A: Yes: she has responsibility for making sure projects are running well, has to consider budgets, make sure the team is motivated, keep her clients happy and manage suppliers.

Q: *Does Paula share the same day-to-day challenges as other people in the community?*

A: Yes: she has similar issues to other IT project managers; for example, she needs to iron out team conflicts, manage expectations with her clients, communicate with other parts of the organisation and negotiate supplier contracts.

Q: *Would Paula be able to learn things from other people in the community that would make her better at her job?*

A: Yes: she is the only project manager on her team and would benefit greatly from understanding how others tackle the same problems that she faces.

Q: *Would people in the community be able to learn things relevant for their day-to-day work from working closely with Paula?*

A: Yes: she has been working in similar roles for a number of years and has learnt a great deal that could be shared with others; she'd be a great person to pair with others to tackle new problems.

Once you start to identify people for whom you can answer "yes" to each of these four questions, you can start building your community.

Don't worry if you don't get it right the first time. You can always improve it as you go. Talk to people, either as a group or one-to-one, to tell them about what you are trying to do and then invite them to join.

It's important to remember that membership of the community should be voluntary. Those that take part should be there because they want to be. Early on in the community's growth some people won't see why they should join, but may do later on. Remain open to them joining later.

6. Becoming a Community

Once you have signed up your first set of community members, it's time to start getting to know each other and forming a sense of community. The most important thing to do as a foundation for a successful community is to start to build trust and social connections between the members. This will lay down a strong base to build upon.

In this chapter we look at:

- a sense of community

- first steps in creating a community

- creating community alignment

A Sense of Community

A community of practice is like any community. It is worth always having in mind the ingredients of a sense of community, which McMillan and Chavis (1986) [18] describe as:

- membership

- integration and fulfilment of needs

- shared emotional connection

- influence

Membership

A feeling of belonging, that members have invested part of themselves to become a member and, therefore, have a right to belong. Clear boundaries in membership create a clear idea of who belongs and who does not, and this leads to a feeling of emotional safety. Other elements that supplement this are a shared language or shared symbols like names for communities or mascots.

Integration and fulfilment of needs

The group must have alignment in order to reinforce members' beliefs. The community must have a sense of togetherness and must be rewarding for its members.

Shared emotional connection

Members must feel emotionally connected to each other through shared or common experiences. This can be encouraged with regular contact and meaningful interactions. Such a connection will create a space for members of the community to be honest with each other and to build trust.

Influence

The members must have some influence over what the group does, and the group must have the ability to influence its members. This helps the members feel ownership over the group and creates alignment between them.

For a community of practice, it is also important that the community has influence within the organisation or the wider network within which it exists. If members know that what they do has a significant long-term effect on their personal and group situation, then they will see value in being part of the community.

First Steps in Creating a Community

Before you first gather you should answer a couple of key questions. This stage provides an opportunity for leaders or core members to get things off to a good start and to help start building connections from the beginning. The questions are:

- what will your members do in the first few sessions?

- when should the community meet?

The first thing you must do is get everyone together. If your group is new, or members don't yet know each other very well, or it has new members or needs reinvigorating, then use icebreaker exercises. Icebreaker exercises create chances for members to find out more about each other and are an easy way to start interacting. They are also a good way to engage people in the session and to get them to stop thinking about other work.

Use icebreaker exercises for the first few sessions or when you think they are relevant to reinvigorate the group. Once the group gets to know each other better and becomes more open, you won't need the exercises as often.

If members are very new to each other – or new to interacting in a community format – use some early sessions to share what you are working on and stories from your week, until you feel the group is trusting enough to tackle details about what you'll do next as a community.

At the very early stage of a community, it's natural that some people will be more engaged than others. Some may come to fewer sessions because of work commitments, or they may be unsure about what the community can offer them. Be open and inclusive by encouraging people to come as often as they can and by rolling out the welcome mat when they do. Even if attendance is low, carry on with the meetings. As others see the benefits, they will join.

There are many icebreakers to choose from, that you can find in books or published on the internet. Below are some examples you could use:

Two truths and one lie: participants tell everyone three things about themselves: two things that are true and one a lie. The group has to guess which is the lie. This is great for starting to get to know interesting things about each other, and can be fun.

Team 'Top Trumps': Everyone takes an A6 piece of card and on it draws a picture of themselves, writes a two to five word bio, writes four skills they have (either work or personal) and awards themselves a score out of ten for each of those skills.

This exercise is great because it helps people in the group learn more about the skills others have outside work. Often people will learn that they have similar interests and hobbies, and so it helps to build interpersonal bonds. It also engages a different part of the brain because players are drawing. I've seen groups get really excited by this part.

Meeting face to face is important for building trust. Where possible, try to get the whole community together to meet. If the entire group cannot meet in one go, find ways for individuals to travel to each other in smaller groups or alone, so that people start to form connections. If this is impossible, find ways to hold less formal sessions using digital tools; it will be more difficult to build bonds this way, but not impossible.

I've found it beneficial to stick to a regular day and time to get together and to book it in everyone's diaries. If the community all works in the same building, book in a weekly face-to-face session. If members are distributed across short distances that involve a couple of hours' travel, book a monthly face-to-face session along with regular video calls. If they are widely distributed, book in regular computer-mediated conversations. If you are having face-to-face meetings, make sure you have the facilities to dial-in people that cannot be in the room but want to take part. If they are travelling a long way, make the best use of any time you have together and build opportunities to be social into your sessions.

It's important to have a regular rhythm for the community so that the members know when to expect to meet up. Let members agree a time to meet that they can commit to. If you can, send a recurring digital calendar invitation, so that the schedule is in everybody's diaries. In addition to this, it's important to allow people time to get to know each other in a more relaxed setting away from their everyday work. Your group should organise lunches or social events to allow for more informal ways of connecting.

Where you should meet?

Don't forget to find the right space to meet. To encourage trust and a feeling of safety, make sure you can be in a space where you can close the door. If your office is like many I have seen, good meeting room space will be hard to book, so booking a regular and repeating slot in advance will be the best way of making sure you have that space for future sessions. It's also worth considering a space to meet away from the office. This will help people engage in sessions away from the shadow of day-to-day work.

Creating Community Alignment

Alignment and shared goals will help your community flourish. When people have a shared sense of direction it helps them to understand where to put their efforts and aligns them to a common cause.

Simon Sinek talks about a 'golden circle' that creates really successful teams and organisations. He suggests they always start with the question "why?" before answering "how?" and "what?"

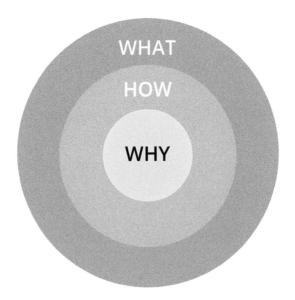

Simon Sinek's golden circle [19]

As members feel more comfortable with each other and start to coalesce into a community, you should start to collectively find out the answers to these questions:

- what is your community vision?

- how will you work together?

- what will you do together?

How quickly your group gets to work on these questions will depend on the community, and whether there are existing relationships between its members.

What is your community vision?

In chapter 5, 'Identifying Who is in the Community', I mentioned that you need a broad vision and initial goals for the community. Having a vision gives the group a shared understanding of why they exist, which helps create common tasks.

If you have already shared something with the members when you initially approached them about joining the community, you can revisit this as a group and start to refine it together. If you didn't start with a vision, now is your chance to create one together.

If you have an existing vision, present it to the group and ask people to comment and feed into it. If you are yet to build one, present why you set the community up, feed-back the needs and benefits, and work with members to build something.

Having a shared vision is a good foundation on which to build your community, so make sure you address this early on.

Your vision for the community should be aspirational, achievable and easy to understand. There are many tools you can use to help build a vision. You'll find ideas in books and on the internet.

One possible workshop format follows four steps.

1: Align the group on what is meant by vision. This will help set the scene and make sure everyone is talking about the same thing.

1.1: Ask the group the question: "What are the qualities a vision should have?" Ask them to individually write their answers on sticky notes, without discussion.

1.2: Ask the group to stick their notes on the wall one by one. Read them out, discuss any differences, then agree a list of qualities.

2: Gather words that are relevant to this group

2.1: Ask the group to write down single words which they think represent for them the group's vision.

2.2: Ask them to stick their notes on the wall one by one and read them out; group them where they are the same or similar in meaning.

3: Share some vision statement examples

3.1: Share some good vision statements with the group. You'll need to find some vision statements that you think are good from other organisations (you'll be able to do this online).

4: Build your vision statement

4.1: Divide your group into teams and ask them to use the words to create a single-sentence vision.

4.2: Present back and discuss, then pick a statement (or combination of statements) that is right for you. Don't worry if it's not perfect: you can tweak it later.

How will you work together?

How you work together covers two factors: your community principles, the rules of how you work together; and your community values, the reason you do what you do.

Community principles

For every group, agreeing principles and ways of working together will help everyone understand how they should treat one another, and how they should expect to be treated.

Work with your community to agree these ways of working and publish the principles somewhere you can all see. They should be owned by the community, so everyone can be accountable for making sure they are followed and call it out when they are not. Revisit them from time to time as a group to make sure they remain relevant.

Creating your principles workshop: an example

There are lots of ways that you could do this, but a fun workshop I have used in the past is the anti-problem, from the book 'Gamestorming: A Playbook for Innovators, Rulebreakers, and Changemakers' [20].

1: What is the worst it could be?

1.1: Give everyone sticky notes and ask them to write down what the worst possible community behaviour would look like; ask them to be as wild as possible and have fun with it.

1.2: Ask the group to stick their notes on the wall one by one and read them out. Group them where they are the same or similar in meaning.

2: How will we behave?

2.1: As a group write down the antidote to each of these behaviours. This is how your community will behave and form its principles.

2.2: Write them up and share them.

Community values

Values are a set of beliefs that members share. Understanding those beliefs will help your members to feel a connection to each other and to the community.

Values can also be used to help explain the community to new or interested members.

Identifying your values workshop: an example

1: Align the group on what is meant by values. This will help set the scene and make sure everyone is talking about the same thing.

1.1: Ask the group a question: What is a value? Ask them to individually write their answers on sticky notes, without discussion.

1.2: Ask the group to stick their notes on the wall one by one and read them out. Discuss any differences then agree a list of qualities.

2: Find out what people's personal values are. This will help to reveal where there is overlap.

2.1: Ask the group a question: What are your values? Ask them to individually write their answers on sticky notes, again without discussion.

2.2: Ask the group to stick their notes on the wall one by one. Read them out and group them into themes

3. Discuss how they match and where they differ

3.1: In smaller groups, ask people to discuss and present back to the other groups a list of five values.

3.2: Discuss the results and agree on a set of shared values which people are happy to sign up to and share with others.

What will you do together?

Now you have a vision statement and principles, it's time to build some goals for the community to help guide what you will do together.

As I mentioned in the chapter on identifying who is in your community, goals should be SMART: Specific, Measurable, Realistic, and Timely. For example:

We will learn about a technique X enough to apply it to a new project within the next three months. We will know we have achieved it when at least two people in the group can report back on their experience of using it.

Or:

We will improve our presentation skills so that members of our community feel confident enough to submit talks to a conference or meet-up in six months. We will know we have achieved this when at least three members have given talks.

Tackling these goals can help you agree what tasks you might do on a regular basis. Once you have your goals, revisit them on a regular basis and create new ones as and when needed.

Create a shared backlog to work against as a team

A backlog is a tool that contains a prioritised list of activity options for the group. When you agree goals and activities, it's a good idea to turn them into a backlog. Online tools like Trello [21] are great for maintaining a community backlog.

Creating your goals workshop: an example

There are lots of ways you could do this. Below is a brief description of one way you could tackle the creation of your goals.

1: Create your goals. You might need a whole session just to do this bit, so give yourself plenty of time.

1.1: Give everyone sticky notes. Ask them to write down what they would like the community to achieve; remind them to think of goals as SMART.

1.2: Ask the group to stick their notes on a wall one by one and read them out. Group them where they are the same or similar in meaning.

2: Prioritising goals. This is so you can focus your efforts on the most important and most impactful goals first.

2.1: Give everyone three sticky dots. Ask everyone to stick one on the goal (or cluster of similar goals) that they think is most important and most impactful. Explain they can use the dots however they wish: one on each, two on one and one on another, or all three on the same goal.

2.2: Place the goals in priority order and confirm that the group is happy with the result.

3: What you could do to achieve the goals. This will give you a chance to create your backlog.

3.1: Break the group into smaller units and divide out the top goals. Ask attendees to discuss what activities the group could do to help achieve each goal.

3.2: Present back to the whole group and discuss. The results will form your community's backlog.

7. Getting Value from Community Interactions

As your members get to know each other, what you use your time together for will help make the community a success. You may have a specific time to meet, but you will also want to supplement that with further community interactions. Your community will need collectively to decide how it will use its time. Make sure that there are plenty of opportunities for:

- building social connections

- learning as a group

- talking, solving problems and building better practices

- sharing outside the community

- creating community improvements

My list is not exhaustive; you will need to adapt what you do to your own needs. But it is a good starting place.

Building Social Connections

Making connections is vital to your sense of community, so make time for people to talk about things other than work. Make your social events inclusive and remember that different members of the community will have different needs and commitments that should be considered. For example, evening events will be fine for some people and not for others. Accept that not everyone will be able to come to everything, so allow for different types of social events. Tools like Doodle [22] are great for scheduling time with people without creating a lot of email traffic.

Learning as a Group

Learning as a group is important for your community to grow and for the development of its members. You will want to create the right environment for inspiring conversation and learning, rather than design a curriculum.

Different types of learning activities that I have seen succeed include:

- presentations and talks
- deliberate practice
- games and workshops
- visits and tours

Presentations and talks

Presentations and talks offer a great chance to introduce the community to new topics and concepts. These can be given by people within the community, people outside the community but within the organisation, or external speakers. Bringing in people from outside the community will add new ideas, opinions and thinking, and so will help keep the community fresh. There are also many opportunities to watch talks that have been recorded at other events or shared on blogs and other websites. TED [23] is just one example.

Deliberate practice

Deliberate practice is a tool that mimics experiential learning in a safe environment. This is a chance to stretch existing knowledge and skills, while introducing feedback loops to accelerate that learning. Deliberate practice can be used to help support skills development in the community as a whole or for smaller groups. This can be done as small projects or within a single session, and can be a great chance for people to learn. I talk about identifying skills gaps in the next chapter, which will give some direction for your deliberate practice.

Games and workshops

Games and workshops can support deliberate practice or introduce new skills or concepts to the community in a less formal way. There are many resources, for example 'Gamestorming: A Playbook for Innovators, Rulebreakers, and Changemakers' [24], Hyper Island Toolkit [25], and TastyCupcakes.org [26]. Games and workshops help people to learn in a less formal environment. They can also give members the chance to practice facilitation within a safe space.

Visits and tours to other places

Visits to other workplaces will help your community members discover ways other people tackle similar challenges in different environments. You can visit places within your organisation, or other places that share similar challenges to you. In turn, you can invite others into your organisation, which offers an external view on how you do things. You could visit places as individuals, small groups or larger groups. Groups benefit from visits because they can discuss what they saw and any ways in which they may incorporate some of that learning into their own way of doing things.

Talking, Solving Problems and Building Better Practices

Make sure you create time for the community to have less-structured meetings where they can discuss things that are on their mind and bring their problems to the community's safe space. This can immediately help others within the community and also highlight areas for which the group may need to consider creating better practices.

You could ask members of the community to propose topics they want to address prior to meeting up, or even use a Lean Coffee [27] structure to build the meeting agenda as you go.

Lean coffee

An agenda-less meeting where participants create and prioritise the agenda as they go, to make it more relevant to the participants.

1: Create options. Participants individually write down what they want to discuss on sticky notes.

2: Vote on topics. Participants then have two votes each on the topics, which creates a prioritised list.

3: Set the agenda. The facilitator divides the meeting into the highest ranked topics and works through the sticky notes in priority order.

Solving problems in smaller groups

Your time to problem-solve shouldn't be restricted to group activities; focused sessions within smaller groups allow people to get deeper into problems. I have found it extremely valuable to pair or buddy people up to work on specific problems (dyads), especially when someone is new to the community or needs additional support.

During their time together, the pair can discuss a particular problem or challenge they are working on. This has proven to be valuable in many ways: it creates better quality, as two people are more likely to pick up mistakes and outliers; it creates better communication and exploration of problems, because two people discuss as they go; it encourages better knowledge retention and transfer, as two people are aware of the problem and solution rather than just one; and it means shorter feedback loops, because solutions are reviewed as they are created.

Taking this concept further, I have found triads (groups of three people) to be even more valuable for ongoing discussion groups, problem solving and learning. The benefits of three people are that: it puts an additional opinion into the conversation, which can help open up options and remove an either/or dilemma; it can help break down any feelings of a mentor/mentee type of relationship, where a pair may always feel that one person knows more than the other; it can help with scheduling, if one person isn't available, then the other person might well be; and it gives an opportunity for observation, where two people can work as a pair and the third can observe then give feedback.

Building Successful Communities of Practice

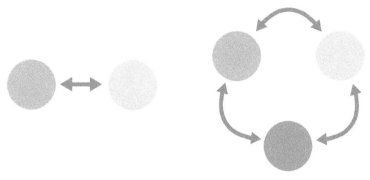

Dyads and triads

Sharing Outside the Community

When a community is mature and members have built strong interconnections, it's a good time to start sharing outside of the community with open door activities, where non-members can join in. This gives the chance for people outside the community to benefit from its knowledge, but retains the safe space of the closed-door activities and members-only interactions.

This is a good opportunity to share community practices with the rest of the organisation and to help bring in new points of view. It also stops the community becoming a silo or echo chamber. Open-door activities can be done through:

- show and tells
- marketing material
- presentations and training
- crossovers with other communities

Show and tells

Showing other people what the community has been working on will give members a chance to celebrate work completed and to share ideas with other people in the organisation.

Marketing material

Posters, leaflets and emails are a great way to show other people what your community does. These can be especially useful if your community is distributed or if you want to create a greater general awareness of what you do.

Presentations and training

Much of what you do will be of interest to people outside of the community. Presenting ideas or training others gives the community a chance to share knowledge in a more structured way and gives the organisation a chance to learn. You can ask people within the organisation what they would most like to know, and base presentations or training on those requests. This will help when someone has asked to join the community, to learn from its members, but does not fit into the membership criteria. It gives you an alternative to offer them.

Crossovers with other communities

Inviting crossover from other existing communities of practice will give your members insight into what other people do — and how their work complements yours and where it crosses over. If other communities exist within your organisation, get in touch and discuss ways to collaborate.

Creating Community Improvements

You should always be looking for ways to improve. To ensure members continue to get value from the community, put aside regular time to review how the community is working together and how it could improve. This will help to keep the community relevant and useful for its members.

Many software teams using agile frameworks use a tool called retrospectives to regularly make team improvements. It's a practice that can easily be replicated for any type of team or community.

The retrospective: an example

There are many forms of retrospective, which you can explore on the Agile Retrospective Resource Wiki [28]. Below is a standard format covering: what went well; what didn't go so well; and how can we improve.

1: What went well. People in the group take five minutes to individually write down things that have been going well in the period since the last retrospective, one thing per sticky note.

2: Post-up. The first person then sticks their own notes on a wall one at a time and briefly talks through them. Someone else then gets up, grouping anything similar and talking through theirs. Repeat until everyone has had a turn.

3: What didn't go well. Repeat step 2 and 3 for what didn't go so well since the last retrospective, then post-up.

4: What can we do to improve? As a group discuss what improvements the group can make and what remedial actions can be taken. Prioritise actions and agree on who will take the three most important forward before the next retrospective.

It is very important that participants in the retrospective feel safe to talk openly. This will give you the best chance to create actions that will make real improvements. As a group, get good at this format of retrospective. Later, start to look for new formats to keep things interesting.

8. Identifying Skills Gaps to Work On

As well as building a backlog of potential improvements, a community of practice can start identifying what skills your community members need to build in order to be better at their job. This could be part of personal development, or can even help if the organisation or community want to build skills that don't currently exist, but which will be needed.

The questions you should consider are:

- what skills are needed in order to do the role?

- what skills do individuals have?

- what skills do individuals want to develop?

- what skills does the community as a whole have?

What Skills are Needed in Order To Do the Role?

If your organisation has job descriptions, these are often a good place to start to answer this question. However, in many places job descriptions are out of date or even mismatched to roles that people are actually doing. Identifying skills in this way will also give you a chance to revisit the job descriptions with people that are actually performing the role.

Gather the community together. Ask members to individually capture everything they do on a regular basis on separate sticky notes. Then ask them one by one to post them on a board and briefly explain each one. Ask them to group anything similar into themes and to discuss if they are part of the role or not. I gather everything up, de-duplicate it, review the themes, clarify some meanings and present it back for comment.

After one or two iterations, we have a good list which can be used for personal skills mapping, identifying what skills are missing, for personal development goals, and for updating future job descriptions.

Once you have an agreed list, ask people to highlight additional skills they have or want that may not seem explicitly related to their role. For example, people might be great at public speaking; this may not be an explicit part of a job description, but would be beneficial.

If your organisation is thinking about expanding a role into a new area, this is also a great time to capture the additional skills your community already has in that area, and ascertain where it might need to expand.

What Skills Do Individuals Have?

Once you have identified the skills people need for their role, you can use this data to do some skills confidence mapping of individuals against it. This exercise should be undertaken with the person rather than about them, as a judgement of their skills set or weaknesses. It should be done with some caution and made clear that it's to support development rather than to assess individuals.

It is important to remember that skills and confidence in skills are not always the same thing. Someone can be very skilled in an area, but if they are not confident in their skills, it will become apparent at skills mapping stage.

To help guide people with their skills confidence mapping, it's useful to use an existing model of skills development. For example, the Five-Stage Model of Adult Skill Acquisition, created by Hubert and Stuart Dreyfus in 1986 [29], defines five stages: expert, proficient, competent, advanced beginner, and novice.

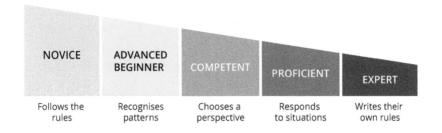

NOVICE	ADVANCED BEGINNER	COMPETENT	PROFICIENT	EXPERT
Follows the rules	Recognises patterns	Chooses a perspective	Responds to situations	Writes their own rules

The Five-Stage Model of Adult Skill Acquisition

When working through individuals' skill levels against the skill-set identified by the community, you can use a model like this to help people rank their own level of skills — from novice to expert — against each of them.

Another tool I have used in skills mapping — less nuanced than the Dreyfus Model — is ShuHaRi, a martial arts term that relates to learning a technique. It breaks down into three stages.

Shu: The protection stage, where the student follows what the master teaches them.

Ha: The breakaway stage, where the student starts to learn the underlying principles and theory behind a technique and begins to integrate learning into their practice.

Ri: The creating stage, where the student creates their own approaches and adapts what they have learned to their own particular circumstances.

Once everyone in the community has repeated this exercise, you will collectively be able to identify where there are gaps and/or low coverage in the community. You can use this information to feed the learning backlog and to hire new skills into the community.

What Skills Do Individuals Want to Develop?

When you have an understanding of how an individual's skills map to those that are needed for a role, you can work with them to help create a personal development plan.

It is important for people not to try and take on all areas they need to improve. They should focus on the highest priority one in the imminent period of time. The discussion about which area is most important can happen between the individual and their line manager or mentor. It should take into account: what skills the individual is most interested in and keenest to develop; what skills they are missing that most affect their ability to do their role; and what skills the community and organisation are most lacking.

The individual can use this top priority to help focus their next development objective. Once they are confident with that skill, they can go back to the list and take on the next highest priority.

What Skills Does the Community as a Whole Have?

Having a community of people who have different skills will help members when it comes to skills development. You now have a skills map of the community and an understanding of where individuals are focusing their personal development. From this you can easily spot potential matches and buddy up people who can learn from each other. You can use this information to help create dyads and triads within your community.

If there is no one else with the skill an individual wishes to develop, they will need to look outside the community for help, either to other people, to self-initiated learning, or to training.

If there is a big gap in the community's skill-set, you can decide to work on this together as a community, add it to your community backlog, and make it a topic for learning sessions. You could consider bringing in external speakers or training for the entire group.

9. Growing the Community of Practice

There are a number of ways in which a community can become more mature. As well as growing membership, the ways in which people connect will become deeper and members will develop ownership of their community. I have already explored ways of using meetings and time together to deepen skills and connections. In this chapter I'll look at:

- growing community membership

- identifying types of members

- identifying and growing community leaders

- growing your community reach

Growing Community Membership

During the initial stages of a community, your membership will be limited to people from your immediate networks and those you can easily reach. As the community grows, you will need to focus additional efforts on growing its membership past just these people.

At this point, the community should have an identity. Others around the organisation will have noticed something is going on, making it easier to reach new members. People may have already approached you and asked to join, but don't worry if they haven't.

To find new members, you may already have a number of tools and resources available within your organisation to help you grow membership. These are: your extended networks, your community's networks and your story.

Things to consider:

- how can existing members get the story out?

- are there formal or informal structures you can use to reach people?

- what marketing tools can you use?

- are there any other people whose help you can enlist?

- making the message easy to understand

How can existing members get the story out?

Your members are the biggest advocates for the community. Ask them to talk about it within their own networks, through email lists, meeting groups or informally. Bring the topic up for discussion in one of your sessions or over a shared communication tool. Ask your group how they can reach new people.

Are there formal or informal structures you can use to reach people?

Is there a line managers' network, or a programme structure through which you can find people? Are there any regular organisational communications, like internal emails, blogs, wikis or social tools?. Are there any formal email lists you can use to reach people? Find the communication channels that your organisation uses, and who manages them. Find a way to present at relevant meetings or write a message to be shared.

Are there any informal groups, like social, sports or activities groups? Are there informal instant message channels or email lists? Find the people who run these groups and ask to talk to their members.

What marketing tools can you use?

Think about ways in which you can reach people who are outside of any other networks, or any ways in which you can use marketing tools. For example, you could create posters to put in high footfall areas or distribute fliers advertising your community in places where you think new members might see them.

Are there any other people whose help you can enlist?

If you are trying to reach a department or area you are less familiar with, can you call on people who know that area better or can put you in touch with relevant people? Find out if anyone in your community has connections, and if you can get an introduction to the right person.

Making the message easy to understand

Don't forget to sell the message about why you exist, what needs you are addressing, how you work together, and what you do. Make it easy for people to self-identify with what you say about community members, so they can easily see how it would benefit them. Give them an easy way to get in touch, create an email address that's easy to remember or a web page prospective members can reach you through.

Identifying Types of Members

Because membership of the community is optional, it is normal for there to be different types of members. You can identify the differences in engagement and effort that they put into the community. This is natural for any community, and the makeup of membership should only be reviewed if it becomes a problem that affects trust or interactions.

Members types are:

- core
- active
- occasional
- peripheral
- outside

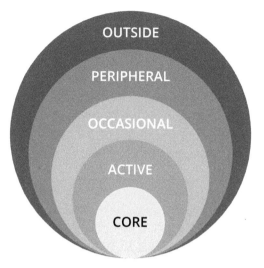

Community member types

Core

Members who lead, coordinate or run community activities. These are the members who make sure people are meeting up and getting the best from the group, and that activities are organised. Without these members, there won't be a community. A small community may consist solely of core members.

Active

Members who regularly join community activities. These are the people you expect to see at regular meetings, being vocal and actively making suggestions about what happens with the group. They will take some ownership of the group. These have the potential to become core members.

Occasional

Members who show up to community activities from time to time, but don't attend every meeting. They will be mostly passive and more likely go along with group decisions than be vocal about community direction. They will take part when it is most relevant to them. Some of them may feel the group is not valuable enough for them to make time; some may be overwhelmed with other work. It's worth spending time with these members to understand the barrier(s) to their becoming an active member.

Peripheral

Members who rarely come to community activities and are very passive. They may also be new joiners that haven't yet been brought into the group, or they may have opted out. If they are new members, it's worth spending time with them to make them feel welcomed into the community. If they have opted out and have little interest in joining in, it's worth exploring if these members can be brought further into the group or not. Always leave room for them to become more active members in the future.

Outside

These are people outside of your community. They may be sponsors, supporters, members of other communities of practice, or just interested people. It might never be relevant for them to be anything more than outside people, but you should think about how to communicate with them.

Identifying and Growing Community Leaders

In order to create a self-sustaining community and encourage ownership of the community by the community, now is a great time to start identifying people who can become core members, help run the community, and share leadership roles.

Natural leaders will already be active members and they will start to identify themselves by the amount of effort and engagement they give to the community. As people start to show their desire to get involved with leadership, let them become part of it. Don't be precious about the need to continue with one leader or core group. If a community is to become self-sustaining, leadership needs to be taken on by the group as a whole and not owned by just one person or one small group.

Consider what the community needs and let emerging leaders take on responsibility for parts of that support. Always be there to give them support and reassurance when they need it.

Growing Your Community Reach

As your community becomes established, more people on the outside start being very interested and want to join in. If they are a fit for your community — using the criteria explained in chapter 5, 'Identifying Who is in your Community' — then welcome them in. If they are not a good fit, you should be cautious about bringing them into your safe environment and upsetting group dynamics.

Often a bad fit will be someone who is keen to learn more from the community, but might not able to bring knowledge in. If a member isn't going to bring anything into the community then it may be best to find other ways to connect with them, rather than disrupt the safe space that your community has created.

To help meet these kinds of needs in the past, I have set up open learning sessions, where members of the community present information and ideas on topics of interest to those outside the community. These sessions are for anyone in an organisation who wants to come along and learn more. They start broadly to explain what roles people in the community perform. I have invited others to identify what they want to know more about and then tailored these sessions to their precise needs.

Where there is crossover knowledge and work with other communities of practice that is important for the organisation, it is a good idea to set up specific sessions for communities of practice to get together with a particular topic in mind.

Your community reach will also extend through the better practices that you create and disseminate. As new ideas are formed and new ways of doing things adopted, your community will have a positive and visible impact on the wider organisation.

10. Self-sustaining Communities of Practice

Communities of practice only exist as long as there is an interest from members in maintaining the group. This is why the practice of regularly inspecting how the well the community is meeting needs — and adapting it to ensure it does — is crucial to a community's survival.

A community will best survive when it becomes self-sustaining and self-organising. Throughout this book, we have covered ways in which to create the right environment for a self-sustaining community to grow and thrive.

Self-organisation comes from a clear understanding of the community's goals and autonomy for the community to help achieve those goals in the way that best fits its members. On regular occasions, the community will need to revisit its vision to see that it is still relevant. It will need to review its goals as they are achieved or to verify they are still appropriate.

The key elements of a self-sustaining community are:

- leadership

- membership

- knowledge and practices

- skills development

- visibility and support

Leadership

Community members are comfortable with the leadership and at nominate and adjust its own leaders and leadership as it needs to.

The community regularly has a clear vision. Members feel connected to it and have the means to change it if needed. The community tracks and renews goals on a regular basis.

Membership

Members are engaged with the community and there are enough core members to maintain focus on the community vision, to organise interactions and to sustain interest in community activities. There is a clear understanding of who belongs in the community. There is a safe environment and real connections exists between members. Members have mutual respect and trust each other.

Knowledge and practices

The community continues to learn on a regular basis and uses the community structure to get better at what they do. The community creates better practices and standards, which they actively share with the organisation. The organisation looks to the community as the experts.

Skills development

The community takes the lead on its members' professional development. It seeks to bring new skills in. Members influence their own skills development.

Visibility and support

The organisation in which the community resides supports the community and its ongoing development. People outside of the community advocate for it.

You will be able to recognise a self-sustaining community by its ongoing commitment and passion from members.

Conclusion

Communities of practice can be a powerful force within your organisation. Supporting the creation of healthy communities will benefit you in many ways. They can support organisational learning; accelerate the personal development of members; enable better knowledge management; improve communication; build better practices; make people happier; break down silos; and facilitate staff hiring and retention.

Like all good things, they take a lot of time and effort to get right. They need ongoing support. But the return on investment is huge and affects many parts of an organisation positively. An early-stage community will need more nurturing and support when it starts to grow.

If you notice a community of practice forming, then see what you can do to support its growth. If you are interested in getting something going, put someone who understands communities in place to help get things going and to build space for the community. Then let the community build itself from there. Use the chapters in this book to help inform your own community's development and to adapt what you learn to your own particular situation.

This book is a first edition based on my wide-ranging experiences supplemented by desk-based research. Over time I expect it to grow, as I learn more through personal experience and talking to others with their own stories to share. If you would like to talk more about your own experience of communities or practice or using this book, please email me at emily@tacitlondon.com

Resources & References

1. Etienne Wenger-Trayner and Beverly Wenger-Trayner. 'Introduction to Communities of Practice'; wenger-trayner.com/introduction-to-communities-of-practice [Accessed 30th November 2015]

2. Jean Lave and Etienne Wenger (1991). 'Situated Learning: Legitimate Peripheral Participation': Cambridge University Press

3. Taiichi Ohno (1988). 'Workplace Management': Productivity Press

4. Albert Bandura (1971). 'Social Learning Theory': Stanford University

5. David A. Kolb (1984). 'Experiential learning: experience as the source of learning and development': Prentice Hall; academic.regis.edu/ed205/kolb.pdf

6. Government Digital Service (2014). 'Training and learning about agile': Government Service Design Manual; gov.uk/service-manual/agile/training-and-learning.html [Accessed 30th November 2015]

7. The Agile Alliance (2001). 'Manifesto for Agile Software Development'; agilemanifesto.org [Accessed 30th November 2015]

8. S. D. N. Cook and J. S. Brown (1999). 'Bridging epistemologies: the generative dance between organizational knowledge and organizational knowing': Organization Science, 10 (4): 381–400

9. Jeanne Meister (2012). 'Job Hopping Is the "New Normal" for Millennials': Forbes; forbes.com/sites/jeannemeister/2012/08/14/job-hopping-is-the-new-normal-for-millennials-three-ways-to-prevent-a-human-resource-nightmare [Accessed 30th November 2015]

10. Andrew J. Oswald, Eugenio Proto, and Daniel Sgroi (2014). 'Happiness and Productivity': Warwick University; warwick.ac.uk/fac/soc/economics/staff/eproto/workingpapers/happinessproductivity.pdf [Accessed 30th November 2015]

11. David G. Allan (2014). 'Google's algorithm for happiness': BBC [Accessed 30th November 2015]

12. Daniel H. Pink (2009). 'Drive, The Surprising Truth About What Motivates Us': Riverhead Books; danpink.com/drive

13. Carol D. Ryff and Corey Lee M. Keyes (1995), 'The structure of psychological well-being revisited': Journal of Personality and Social Psychology, Vol 69(4), Oct 1995, 719-727

14. Etienne Wenger, Richard McDermott and William M. Snyder (2002). 'Cultivating Communities of Practice: A Guide to Managing Knowledge': Harvard Business School Press

15. Bruce Tuckman (1965). 'Developmental sequence in small groups': Psychological Bulletin, Vol 63(6), Jun 1965, 384–399

16. Martin Webster. 'What Is Matrix Management? — A Guide to Matrix Management: Leadership Thoughts'; leadershipthoughts.com/matrix-management [Accessed 30th November 2015]

17. Henrik Kniberg (2014). 'Spotify engineering culture part 1': Spotify Labs; labs.spotify.com/2014/03/27/spotify-engineering-culture-part-1 [Accessed 30th November 2015]

18. David W. McMillan and David M. Chavis (1986). 'Sense of Community: A Definition and Theory': Dr David McMillian; drdavidmcmillan.com/article-1 [Accessed 30th November 2015]

19. Simon Sinek (2011). 'Start with Why: How Great Leaders Inspire Everyone to Take Action': Penguin

20. Dave Gray, Sunni Brown and James Macanufo (2010). 'Gamestorming: A Playbook for Innovators, Rulebreakers, and Changemakers': O'Reilly Media; gamestorming.com [Accessed 30th November 2015]

21. Trello; trello.com [Accessed 30th November 2015]

22. Doodle scheduling tool; doodle.com [Accessed 30th November 2015]

23. TED; ted.com/talks [Accessed 30th November 2015]

24. Dave Gray, Sunni Brown and James Macanufo (2010). 'Gamestorming: A Playbook for Innovators, Rulebreakers, and Changemakers': O'Reilly Media; gamestorming.com [Accessed 30th November 2015]

25. Hyper Island Toolkit: Hyper Island; toolbox.hyperisland.com [Accessed 30th November 2015]

26. TastyCupcakes.org: Fuel for Innovation and Learning; tastycupcakes.org [Accessed 30th November 2015]

27. Lean Coffee; leancoffee.org [Accessed 30th November 2015]

28. Agile Retrospective Resource Wiki (2013); retrospectivewiki.org [Accessed 30th November 2015]

29. Hubert Dreyfus and Stuart Dreyfus (1986). 'Mind Over Machine: The Power of Human Intuition and Expertise in the Era of the Computer': (New York: The Free Press, 1986), p. 50

Appendix

Identifying community development stage

The Community of Practice Maturity Model can help identify where your community is in its development and what you need to help move it towards becoming a self-sustaining community of practice. It is also available to download at tacit.pub/copmaturitymodel

POTENTIAL

LEADERSHIP

Someone has identified a need and wants to create the community

Leader(s) have time to dedicate to forming the community

Leader(s) have an initial vision and/or goals for the community

MEMBERSHIP

There is an initial criteria for membership

There is an initial list of potential members

Potential members have been asked to join the community

KNOWLEDGE / PRACTICES

Knowledge or practice gaps may have been identified and reflected in the goals

SKILLS DEVELOPMENT

Skill gaps may have been identified and reflected in the goals

VISIBILITY / SUPPORT

There is some organisational support for the community

Visibility is only among those that have been told about it

FORMING

LEADERSHIP

Leader(s) are engaging and motivating members to take part

Leader(s) are setting the standards for what "good" looks like

Leader(s) are beginning to represent members outside of the community

MEMBERSHIP

Members are meeting regularly

Membership extends to the network of the leader(s)

Members understand the criteria for being a member

Members have agreed ways of working and collaboration tools

Members have closed-door (members-only) meetings

Members' initial needs have been identified

Members are beginning to build trust with each other

KNOWLEDGE / PRACTICES

Members are sharing knowledge through stories of their daily work and challenges

Members are beginning to identify their knowledge and practice gaps

SKILLS DEVELOPMENT

Members are beginning to identify their skill gaps

VISIBILITY / SUPPORT

There is some visibility that a community is forming

There is an increase in participation and energy among members

Members make time to dedicate to the community

MATURING

LEADERSHIP

Leadership is shared among a core group; roles and responsibilities are understood

The community has a clear and understood vision and goal agreed by is members

Members are able to influence community direction and activities

MEMBERSHIP

Membership has reached further than the leader's network, people ask to join

There are open-door activities with people outside the community

There are smaller knowledge-sharing groups within the community

Members have a safe and respectful environment, and deal with bad behaviour

Members actively advocate for the community

Members' needs are being met by the community

KNOWLEDGE / PRACTICES

Tools are in place for members to share knowledge

Members are regularly reflecting and adapting community activities

The community creates new practices and shares them outside of the community

The community has a shared backlog of work

Interactions are varied and build trust, create learning, solve problems and share knowledge

The community brings in external knowledge on a regular basis

SKILLS DEVELOPMENT

The community creates or agrees with the job description for the role

The community actively seeks out skills development from within and outside of the community

Members' professional development is supported by the community

VISIBILITY / SUPPORT

The community and its outputs are very visible to the organisation

SELF-SUSTAINING

LEADERSHIP

Leadership responsibilities are distributed throughout the community

The vision and goals are regularly updated by the community

MEMBERSHIP

Members are engaged; the community is part of their normal routine

The community is responsible for hiring into the role and / or community

The community is able to measure and share its successes

The community on-boards new members

KNOWLEDGE / PRACTICES

The wider organisation looks to the community to answer questions

Members actively share standards and practices with the organisation

The community manages its explicit and tacit knowledge

SKILLS DEVELOPMENT

The community is responsible for its members' professional development

VISIBILITY / SUPPORT

The community is an established part of the organisation

People outside of the community advocate for it

About the Author

Emily Webber is an Agile consultant and coach who works with clients on coaching, mentoring, development and training to support Agile delivery and lasting transformation through her organisation Tacit (tacitlondon.com).

She is passionate about helping organisations from small startups to large government departments, working with stakeholders, teams and individuals to help them reach their full potential and develop a culture of continuous improvement. She works to create meaningful connections between people and builds communities to foster learning.

She has been interested in communities throughout her professional and personal life. She built an online community of place in east London (yeahhackney.com). She set up communities of interest around topics such as Agile development (agileonthebench.co.uk). She has also built professional communities of practice within organisations, most notably the Government Digital Service Agile delivery community, founded while she was also in the role of Head of Agile Delivery.

Thank you page

I wrote this book in an Agile and iterative way [see tacit.pub/agilebookwriting], and wouldn't have been able to without my reviewers.

Thanks to: Matt Ballantine, Jack Collier, Jeff Foster, Julie Hendry, Emma Hogbin Westby, Johanna Kollmann, Adam Maddison, Kushal Pisavadia and Mr Santi

My designer, sounding board and husband: Stephen Walker and the team at Drew London.

And everyone along the way who has inputted in some way to my thinking or who will do in the future.

CPSIA information can be obtained
at www.ICGtesting.com
Printed in the USA
BVHW051238300520
580415BV00006B/329